Fractured Lollipop

Poems of Brokenness, Healing and Hope

Mary Anne Abdo

DEDICATION

For those in the social services sector who work tirelessly and compassionately for their clients. Thank you for all that you do for our communities. In memory of my dad, who always taught his children to work hard and to follow our dreams.

Author's Note

As this is a poetry book, there may be some content that is sensitive for some readers. Content disclaimer for reader discretion: Adult Themes.

If you or someone or you know is in need of mental health services, and support I have included resources on page 69.

Table of Contents

Acknowledgments

I am grateful to the editors of the following publications in which many of these poems have appeared:

Bindweed Magazine Winter Wonderland 2022: "Confusion." Summer Madness 2023:"Labyrinth." ❖

The Edge of Humanity Magazine: "It Never Ends," "I Am Me," "Generational Poverty in Three Voices," "The Year of Four Dwellings," and "The Fluidity of Love and Not Hate."

Calla Press Spring Edition 2023: "The Alchemy of Kindness."

Proofreading: Margaret Zelsnack

Photography: Mary Anne Abdo

Jane Stahl Studio, B in Boyertown, Pennsylvania, thank you for taking a chance on my work. Craig Czury, thank you for teaching me that poetry are words woven together like a spider's web and are captured onto the page for the entire world to read.

For my husband, Tom, thank you for all of the love, patience, support, and for enabling my dreams come to reality. For my mom, my children and siblings. I am so blessed to have a wonderful support team.

Battle of the Mind

I find myself in battle pictures of the past, haunting the deepest
recesses of thy soul.
Seeing porcelain as a child, unable to understand why.
Bang after bang hitting young bones,
I stop and wonder after the passage of time.
Why?

An innocent child caught in the middle of that long ago rage, pent
up inside of you.
While she pays the price, the price of your childhood shame.
Appearances are deceiving after these many decades.
The two faces of grace have been played out on the public stage.
One in absolute horror and one so holy.
Who are you really?

One will really never know.
The first of your offspring still endures that tongue of barbed wire
remarks.
Children should never see porcelain so close to the naked eye.
Contemplating over the reason why, does existence really mean
anything?
The brain hurts, the soul goes to and fro in many needless
directions.
Why?

You do not even fathom the depths of how many drownings were
hidden in that closet.
Only our patriarch reached out towards the end;
he understood the pain.
And in a flood of regretful tears, reached out in forgiveness.
Yet forgiveness has been tried and tried again.
Only to be scorned with backbiting words.
Revisiting my battlefield is not a worthy gesture.

I am torn apart—
Please let me escape this single parental storm.
Why?
Your loving words have fallen silent.

Rain

No one sees and yet I hide,
escaping the torment at harried pace.
Not wanting to be human in this humanistic world.
The willow tree and raindrops are the only options.

Wash the old soul away, envisioning with prismatic colors the
newness.
Trying to see through an enveloping darkness from within.
Looking at invisible forgiveness,
somehow the rain mends the tears of searching.

For other places and finding none.
Confusion and self-doubt have sewn,
the seeds of hollowness.
Hearing the baby bird singing amongst the raindrops.
Soothing music as the bird chirps softly.
Amid drops of water pitching against a windowpane.

Remembering days when seeking that pure countenance.
And not being such a hollow shell—
Looking ahead, moving forward one step at a time.
Forgiveness must be found within the writer.
And nowhere else…

Transfer State

The room has no direction; sometimes it is moving wall against
wall.
Clean lines with no blaring reality,
just objects of no valuable meaning or space.
From the sofa of escape—
Until a door has opened the needing to flee onto my bed.
Escaping responsibility, to truly escaping a hole of nothingness.
Objects invoke memories of what was and should have been.
Journeys never taken—
Too scared to leave what false comfort envelops inside those
horrible thoughts.

Which shall it be, pretend everything is fine or just drive away?
Thoughts that sometimes relive themselves over and over again.
Help should be on the way.

Humans are supposed to articulate a rescue but don't really want to
comprehend.
Chin up buttercup.

This will all go by the wayside.
Oh God, get your mental incapacity out of my sight,
closing and seeking a better view.
Wanting to truly breathe.
Binding oneself away from the cushioned objects of no man's
land.

Instigator

One thought, one word, multiple actions.
Anger has a way of destroying someone's soul.
Red pieces the center of your eye while losing all control.
A leather strap holding up trousers,
became the weapon of crying silence—
Overreaction to the untidiness of articles of clothing.
The dampness surrounding retro avocado green-patterned dishes
was a setoff.
Getting your own way seeing the strap welt on our skin while
paying no mind.

Sore point of happiness sitting inside a holy box.
Confessing to the point it became a habit every seven days.
Without fully realizing what damage had been done.
When a lad tried to leave this earth twice.

Yet the other lingers for the sake of her mission to be fulfilled in
prose.
One thing will be understood; trauma and heartbreak linger among
the daisy patch.
The bard holds a daisy while gleefully running through the stillness
of black coalfields.
Forever consoling with great compassion the little, great, blue-eyed
wonder.

Wide Awake on the Fifth of January

Sitting and listening ever dislocated from this insane world.
Winter should have arrived.
Instead an early summer-like day hailed my lunchtime freedom.
I am dreaming through this ambedo moment.
Watching London Town within Wembley Stadium that went live.
For my heart's stereo listens innocently.
Alone with U-2.
The band is the story of life.
My life—
They have serenaded me through failure.
Brokenness—
And never-ending triumph.
Hearing Paul's words as he sings,
and I sing even louder.
A secret not shared, a gift from my father.
Time is slowly disappearing.
Just as the sorrow of December.
Looking up as those clouds of the Holy Spirit
surround that sphere of blue.
And winter's lace trees sway.
As if they were singing in harmonious rhythm.

Fractured Lollipop

Oh so perfect and yet not perfect at all.
Torn and twisted like the bleached white paper encircled, holding
up that lemon lollipop.
Cracked and fractured after that first bite,
pieces falling onto the pavement.

The pieces of a child's understanding.
Gone, trying to comprehend what just happened.
Crouching down in agony of someone's misplaced love.
Still trying to understand what love is truly supposed to be.

Mistrust, lost confidence quietly holding my true self.
Silently brimming with self-loathing.
Bite by every condemning bite—
Putting on the pretend happy face for the world to perceive no
affliction exists.

One half of the brain still grapples with the silence of unwanted
ordeals.
The other half sees light through a childlike imagination.
Always trying to breathe without sinking into the chasm.

Ruth's Place

Human Services internships will awaken you to the flipside
of your cozy life.
Thirty days of sleeping on makeshift beds.
Head-to-head with strangers that seem half dead.

Societies lost and broken beings.
Women telling stories of their hardcore lives.
Sometimes eating food from trash bins and leftover restaurant
scraps, walking all hours of the day and night.

Just wondering and wandering through city streets.
Stories of past idyllic and not-so-happy lives.
Promises made and promises shattered while sleeping in the cold.
Committing a misdemeanor is the only means of a warm jail cell
for the winter.
Hoping the lawyer will intervene—
Sending us to a shelter.
Hearing of a place near Pennsylvania Avenue that provides the
basic needs.
Social workers, volunteers and interns trying to change this broken
system.
Words of encouragement.
Trying to make us more human again.

Labyrinth

Nothing but nothing.
I extinguish my fear of birds flying into the night of no return.
Chalk on the sidewalk washing away those fears.
Bees are consumed with my flower's yellow heart.
The glistening of bodily gestures reveals a true intention.
Masking away the tears of that girlish soul.

Fog never really goes away on a winter's night.
Memories of faraway places thirst for recollection.
Wounds of the long-ago past run away like a pack of wolves.
A faceless mask blows away like a hurricane-force wind,
revealing my true nature.

Gilded, fragmented words turn into mud along the stony cracked
wall.
Writing along the riverbank while a fisherman is casting his line.
Where the words fall into sentences enveloping the bass's wide
mouth.
Universal desires only want silence.
Away from this maddening world of needless motion.

Black darkness creeps in during the howling silver moon.
My body is lost along a myriad of shadows.
Stretching through the Sahara Desert.
Escaping backwards somewhere through that serpentine path.
❖

Riley

Our mischievous little imp.
Fitting in the palm of my hand.
Saved by our Inion from the depths of a city dump.
Named after an Irish lass from the west coast of Ireland.
Eighteen years being our delight.
Beautiful gray, black, tan and hints of white.
Our striped feline imp.
Selfish, not wanting you to leave that warm window perch.
The sunshine warming your sickly body.
Not wanting to bring you to God on my birthday.
Easter Sunday changed everything my dear little one.
For I could no longer bear the suffering to go on.
Tonight and tomorrow morning we will spend our last hours
together.
As you cuddle on my lap.
And gently run my fingers over your delicate fur.
Remembering those days of purrs over tuna treats.
Snuggles—
Talking to birds on the porch and being my sporty girl.
Playing with your tinfoil ball.
Playful sister to Raquel, Dusty and Pumpkin
Giving everyone such joy.
My girl, we will miss you.
As you walk over that colored bridge.
Where no pain exists, our sweet girl.
Experiencing only happiness.
The happiness of being our cherub,
and watching over us all.

Ponderance

Why do we forsake ourselves to fulfill our own material needs?
Why in our world is there never enough time in our day?
When enough time was already given to us!
What does anger have to do with love?
Why does your stress cause someone else pain?
What will it take to change your mind about someone who is
different?
From what we call, "normal society"?
Why are we so quick to judge and find it hard to forgive?
Why do we deny our soul's true calling?
Did you ever think how much unnecessary hurt we have caused
each other?
Just think for a moment and breathe.

I Am Me

We want your vote; the number and the polls count to get your candidate in office.
But I am more than a Democrat or Republican, Conservative or Liberal.
I am more than just a number—

I am a person with thoughts, hopes, feelings and dreams.
I am me with a conscience on how I feel about what is right and what is wrong.
I will not judge, be critical or insult for any agenda.
I will state my facts in the most humanly way possible.
An honest measure to the best of my abilities and expect nothing more but respect.

Words and actions when directed in a manner of arrows,
only defeat the real purpose of our human existence.
Our real purpose loves human interaction that has been bestowed on us by our creator.

What hurts us, hurts our creator in ways the profundity of these feelings, words could never express.
So as we reflect on what these past few years have done to our country, are we more divided than ever?

Is all this bickering worth the loss of civility?
Why can we not learn from one another without fear of judgment or ridicule?
At least if we learn something from each other's culture or viewpoint.
Even if we do not agree with it,
Be human enough to respect it.

I am me—
Do I dare share that with you?

Invisible

Slipping that long white coat on before the bell tolls the eight strike of mourning.
The sorrow for now of bygone glory and missed talents for the sake of keeping finances above water.
I sit on oh so many floors with no home for stability.

People look at my countenance like a thorn in their society.
So fake, so plastic, reminding myself on a daily basis I am not present for their amusement.
But for those people who need it the most.
The outcasts of our society grow in numbers—
Greed, a hurting heart, no home, a lost soul yearning to be fixed in some way.

It is those people in my social worker heart that I try to comfort.
With words of hope, encircled with a smile.
We have no idea the amount of simple kindness, which can turn anyone's day around, even lives around.
Sometimes invisibility is a good thing.
It brings humility for my sake and a sense of hope for humanity.

The Journeys We Plan and the Journeys We Seek

We dream about journeys throughout our lives.
Some journeys are planned with months of preparation.
Time, money and the perfect destination.
Soaking up what this world has to offer.
White sand beaches…
Mountains of no return…
Lush green forests…
Deserts painted against the sky…
Cliffs of white chalk…
The journeys we make are those of expectations.
But unplanned journeys are the heart's true desire.
To trek upon this world without needing a dime.
Finding new places in unexpected realms.
Near our own backyard.
Meditation by the river…
Walking amongst the butterfly parade…
Sitting high on top of the world…
Watching trees form intricate branch patterns…
Deer gracefully walking with their fawns…
We have a choice—
Either taking a rushed pace,
or just letting the journey unburden us.
In a dimension where time is nonexistent.

Harrowing

Chained on a hamster wheel it mimics the current state of
American life.
Running as if living in Manhattan through the streets of Scranton.
I am going to nowhere land—
Punching a time clock through this life and thinking back.
Where did this time go?

Trying to carve time through the layers of responsibility.
Feeling the effects as a member of the in-between generation.
Responsible children for a parent and yet responsible parent for
children.
Deadlines that really never end and destinations scheduled not of
my choosing.
Midday arrives.

Where I am?
Spewing numbers that make no sense.
While spinning the wheel of desperation.

Confusion

Stuck in a corner, the mind and the voice will not scream.
Twisted like a curled-up rubber band.
The thoughts and the attacks never seem to cease.
The dark one tries his hardest to infiltrate my very being.
Trying to destroy every scrap of a peaceful life.
Turning and turning in every way to regain sanity.
Beating my chest for solace,
this is my soul's test.
How far and long will this continue?
Did I throw in the towel and give up the fight?
Never!
Giving up means giving into that deep void.
Its painful edges remind me to forge ahead.
My dearest ones need perseverance for their own peace of mind.
Human contemplation recalls that our crosses can be difficult
amongst the darkness of this world.
Love is the first ingredient in the relief of suffering.
Love, love and love for it is why we are created.
Forgive, forgive and forgive again, until your heart finally melts.
Believe in yourself for I believe in the true potential of everyone's
soul.
❖

Sometimes We Cry

A morning can be like any other morning.
The peering of half-opened eyes as the sun beckons its call.
But schedules we require ourselves to keep.
There are routines that can drive one crazy.
When expectations are not met—

Expectations can be forced upon our children.
Be on time, get up and get on with your day within seconds.
It is a modern concept that parents agitate over and over again.
Which can cause the worst case of the Monday morning blues.
Guilty as charged with this crime today.

Remorse has set in over my actions.
Patience and love must set the tone of our day and not the human
time clock.

Tears Upon My Heart

Where has the innocence of our children gone?
Shrouded amongst the spoils of materialism and the filth of mass communication.
Has produced absolute chaos and confusion.
Find for me the days when a child was in awe over just being a child.
No pressure, no fear, no pain.
Find for me the days when innocence was never corrupted and childhood was sacred.
My heart, my heart is in mourning—

The child's voice needs to be heard for they are crying in the streets.
If we continue to ignore the signs and let denial take us.
Where is the future?

Aspire

Aspire for greatness humbly, for respect will follow you.
Aspire for greatness in haste and you have gained nothing in the end.
The modern world tells us a slow, steady pace is the hardest path.
But indeed the slowest path drinks in our true calling.
The modern world tells us silence is deafening.
Solitude is a gift that we seldom unwrap.
Opening us to one's self fosters creativity and self-respect.
Just listen to your inner voice.

Undercut Moments

Ignoring your insults.
Awkward silence.
Making you wonder about those statements.
Walking away from calamity.
Taking a pause.
Assessing the surface meanings.
Having a difficult time.
Getting to the marrow of it all.
Breathe work and meditation.
Obtaining my heart-center.
Finding grace for us.
Allowing the offender to step back,
think and retract.
Somehow and maybe somehow,
find a mutual empathetic commonality.

It Never Ends

An afternoon breeze moving the wind chimes to and fro.
It echoes the sounds of cardinals and other birds in the distance.
And yet, as the flurry of air rushes by.
So does the screaming echo of the ambulance surrounding my
block.
Another person has fallen to gun violence.
Tears streaming down my face with hearts twisting and turning.
It is all too much.
Victims—
Families of victims.
School lockdowns.
Movie theatres with live terror.
Places of worship.
Malls—
Parades—
Need I say more?
All stopping and praying.
For these senseless acts of inhumanity to cease.
Please tell me, what does this all do?
No one is listening to humanity's pleas.
Of innocent victims lying scattered all around.
Police helicopters hover over my block.
In a time where sometimes we can't even fathom.
An eerie silence has grown while butterflies are dancing across the
lawn.
Nature reminding us there is a better way,
To peacefully coexist.

Retirement Is Not So Golden

Homelessness has risen amongst those who have worked all
their lives.
For they say the golden years are grand.
When some have chosen between their heart medication or their
heat.
For they say the golden years are grand.
When some have no choice but to sell all of their priceless family
artifacts just to survive.

For they say the golden years are grand.
When they are forced to move from the place they called home.
Only to live in cars and trucks with their bulldog in the front seat.
Hoping to find another permanent shelter.
For they say the golden years are grand.
In a country where wealth is predominantly obscene—

And yet disparity is more predominant for many.
For the golden years are not so grand.

The Fluidity of Love and Not Hate

The fluidness of love is captured in crystal clear waters.
A simple element we humans tend to forget.
Water is everywhere.
And yet we seldom look for this expression of love.
Oh, how clear our love for each other would be?
I don't want or need to engage in all of this hate
It is beyond a blinding sight.
I heard the Lark Buntings cry—

At the vision of more bloodshed and bodies underneath white
sheets.
They are now soaring past the heights of their unimaginable pain.
For their love was abundant as water.
We just need to open our hearts and minds.
In acceptance of our wondrous reflections within that fluid crystal
water.

Generational Poverty in Three Voices

Grandmother
Always the rebel hippie, playing the cool girl, smoking a jay with
the boys.
Finding myself pregnant after a night's fling.
Old-fashioned parents none too pleased.
Kicking me out to sleep on a friend's couch.
Crying baby with diapers and no money.
Making myself comfortable in the welfare line.
Not knowing if we could survive.

Daughter
I am the product of a one-night stand.
Angry with this situation.
No mother was ever at home.
Never to guide me from this wretched world.
Vodka being my choice of escaping.
Hungry and alone—
Bullied at school.
Because of no family for me at home.
Hiding amongst the veil of shame.
A sometimes visit from my grandparents.
Social workers and street friends I guess are family.
Sitting in a hospital bed, just gave birth to a daughter.
Waiting on a call from the county assistance office.
And nowhere to go.

Granddaughter
I was born shaking from alcohol withdrawal.
Mom runs away from time to time.
Needing to escape from her pain.
Making sure I am never truly alone.
Grandma is more involved; she is ten years sober.
Taking me to school, soccer and ballet.
Mom just sits by and watches in a trance.
Angry and sad…
Probably wishing she had more of grandma than I have.

At least we eat dinner together.
I think life is getting slightly better.

Together
Sometimes we are dealt cards not of our own choosing.
Seeking emotional support and finding none.
Seeking food and shelter in a never-ending line of disgust.
Wondering when it will be our time.
Wondering why we did this or that.
Hoping each generation's life will be different

Trenches of Life

Sitting in the octagon shade.
Constructed of bricks, glass and steel.
Gazing out into the Hill Section.
Admiring my forty-five minutes of freedom.

Gasping for real air without that regulation mask.
Taking in the beauty of those carved-out, manicured lawns.
And perfectly placed trees.
Pleasing to the eye all year long.
A longing to end the madness of this technological world.
Stuck behind many desks and running onto every floor.

To really sit underneath cherry and red maple trees.
Upon that old park bench.
Without paying attention to human-manufactured time
Oh, mercy me.
All these trees and no time to comprehend silence.

Disposable Feelings

Not wanting to intrude on your day.
Asking a question for assistance.
Hearing me and not really hearing me at all.
Acknowledgment ignored—
Words never spoken to express an honest assessment of my thoughts.
Are now gone into obscurity.
Yet I stand in front of you as an invisible image that has been tossed aside.
Disposable comes to mind like litter on the street.
Technology has invaded our society to make human beings not so human.
Hiding behind the masks of glass screens and cell phones.
Saying and typing what we want without consequence.
Not realizing feelings are not meant to be disposable.
Losing the art of human connection and communication.
The ability to look into someone's eyes and understand the true meaning of their unique humanity.
Is slowly going by the wayside.
No wonder deep mental pain is felt by all walks of life.
We are not meant to be disposable, instead we are meant for appreciation.
No matter what we bring to the table of life.

Keystone Mission

Pandemic poverty has hit the streets.
Begging for government grants—
Trying to sustain poverty's demands.
One line on Olive Street with offerings of three square meals.
Another line for social services aid along Pine Brook.
Our mission at Keystone is simple.
Provide hope and help to the homeless.
The hungry and those who are hurting.
Covid-19 brought so many hurting and hungry.
Once thriving human beings are reduced to empty shells.

Jobs lost—

Food security lost—

Shelter lost—

Families lost—

Friends lost—

Addiction recovery lost—

Mental stability lost—

Roaming from street to street.
Winding up in tent cities by the expressway.
Wondering why.
And how.
Trying to change.

Just trying—
Counselors and volunteers meeting the needs at hand.
Helping to pursue life-changing transformations.
Genuinely building trust.

Moment by moment.
Step by step.

Words, Words, Words

Words, the great and powerful muse used throughout millennia.
Whose powers fly away as the nightingale mind races, dreaming of
the morning sun.

Feather pens and parchments are placed on the whitewashed wood.
Diagramming the correct noun to pronoun as Sister Clare Ann
pronounced.
Without needing to rhyme—

Always searching that cranial computer for new words: meaningful
words, nonsensical words, opposite words, smashed words,
animated words, mirthful words and words of my own accord.
If a certain pedagogue could read this now.
For the words fell out of their lips.
The academics achieved would certainly not set this world on fire.

The Year of Four Dwellings

Ultimatum given, but you never sought to heed a word.
Nowhere to turn after three decades and three years.
After many agonizing tears.
Leaving behind the home on Center Street because of your lack of unity.
Political aspirations and entailments were more important.
Moving up to the middle of Rock Street, with clothes and cats in tow.
Leaving for work the next day in absolute angst.
While putting on that fake smile for the entire world to see.
Sure the Rock had more than enough amenities of that former home.
What a switch—
A parent having to move in with a child.
In order to escape his father.
Watching the stars poolside, smelling the sweet smoke of steak.
Happily trying to gain some sort of self.
Only to be ripped away again.
Fleeing from an unpleasant encounter.
Driving so fast with clothes and cats in tow.
Now the child must live with her parents.
Something that was left behind thirty-three years ago
How could this be happening?
Scaled back dwelling place, sharing the room with a sibling.
Sleeping on an inflatable bed hidden in a corner.
No privacy to grieve—
No yard to tend lost flower and vegetable gardens.
Being bombarded with questions.
Hearing my mother's tears and pleas to go back.
While my dad's anger over his pending death permeated every room.
Smells of 1970s recipes wafted around the apartment.
Feeling ever so trapped. Trying to make sense.
While nothing makes sense of why divorce is so cruel.

Loss of love—

Loss of self—

Loss of family—

Loss of friends—

Loss of home—

Finally solace in a long-lost childhood acquaintance.
Moving yet again with clothes and cats in tow.
To a familiar ancestral neighborhood near Philo.
This place of refuge still provides the peace.
Where pretense does not exist.
It is where Lebanese food and culture are celebrated.
It is where woodland creatures dwell and are fed and admired.
It is where the porch is a gathering place for all.
It is where creativity has no bounds.
It is where true love resides.
Surely this is my final stop before the heavenly destination.

Aaliyah and Thaddeus

Vacating my mind and soul a respite created in escaping the
burden of a lost childhood.
Two faithful companions sojourn through this existence called
occupied movement.
Getting the feeling of being on this earth,
and yet really not belonging to this blue planet.

Out-of-body experiences enable the intellect to wander away from
this world and move to an empyreal one.
If only for a few precious moments a kaleidoscopic view of
circulating color.
Seeing through heaven's two white lights, guiding me to what lies
ahead.
Beauty my dear beauty; never forget who you truly are.
This dimensional sphere is a staged fallacy.
A tugging pull between man's perceptions of control.
And the all-encompassing love of our eternal guidance.

Ripples of Aging

The Four Geniuses of Life—

Adventurous Childhood,

Transitional Youth,

Middle Hill Mentors,

and Enduring Wisdom.

Exchanged pleasantries on nature's weathered oak boat.
Gliding along lake silver water.
Underneath the wild Adler tree.
In the dark night of a crescent moon.

Reflections of an enchanting, dreamy painting.
Floating into the light of twinkling fireflies.
Majestic white owls covered the four geniuses with
spiritual wisdom.

Adoring the verses of each seasonal equinox.
An extraordinary sight as the chimes tolled eleven-eleven.
Life is a process of adventure, transition, mentorship and wisdom.
Having moments of courage.

Glorious and gorgeous moments—
Being an authentic spiritual being.
Finding resilience in the face of hardships.
Engaging the present while releasing the past.
Always dreaming about the future.

Silence

Getting into the deep crevasse of our souls.
Our very being craves what is not always heard.
Stifling ourselves with modern noise to drown out what is interior.
Sitting here breathing, wondering how to obtain nothing.
Needing to find life richer and fuller.
Having a conversation with our unknown.
Hearing nature's world, which is always true.

Earth—

Moving—

Waves cresting.
Birds singing.
Sand granules shifting.
Snow becomes water.
Monkeys swinging from trees.
Camels resting in silence.
Intimate stillness within the forest.
Trees swaying in the breeze.
Streams merging into rivers.
Flowers opening and closing.
Whales breathing underwater.
Golden wheat rustling.
Horses galloping.
Harmonious alive.

Stars—

Shining—

Give me silence in this exquisiteness.
A silence of contemplative radial change.

The Land of Make Believe

Children have fascinating ways of making up games,
and magical stories.
Spontaneously running through the park,
and swinging on a swing.
Creating journeys of riding wild horses,
in a circus ring.
Using their imaginations while painting watercolor streams.
Twirling and giggling as one wishes until they are dizzy.
Building impromptu tent cities in the yard.
Pretending their angel guides are eating lunch with them.
And wishing on a star.
While the moon gobbles up the cheese.
Being off the cuff with the details of their day.
Always adventurous without restraint.
Singing songs of unrehearsed melodies.
Making up improvisational tales to childhood friends.
Splashing about, with dinosaurs in a wading pool.
Picking up buttercups to see if their chins turn yellow.
Hauling their dolls and collected rocks,
in little red wagons.
Waiting for the ice cream truck to always appear.
Oh, how my dreams wander to these childhood memories.
Making the land of make believe ever so vividly real.

Questioning Events

Admittance to long-term care.
Final downsizing tasks.
Accumulation of meticulous notes.
Lifetime of memories.
Books of family recipes.
Books you published.
Photos fading to brown.
Large clothing donation bins.
Selling your car.
Driving to Goodwill.
Making other arrangements.
Ups and downs expected.
Nieces helping out.
Apartment keys turned in.
Closing a door.
On a life that matters.

Last Phone Call

One call, four lines.
Dad, can you hear us?
Mom is outside of your bedroom window.
She wants to say, hello!
Hearing his wife banging on the window.
Can you hear me?
Only an inaudible acknowledgement rang over the receiver.
Statements of love mixed with cracked voices of sorrow.
Covid had stolen yet another family's human touch,
to soothe a dying man.
Word, tears and a garbled,
"I love you," came from his lips—
Knowing in our hearts this call was Dad's last goodbye to us.
Via a phone and a nursing home window.
Yes Covid…
You have swallowed our world's freedoms to your smarmy
delight.
Now those left behind must pick up the tattered pieces.

Distractions

A very cold day for a memory.
Looking out a large picture of glass.
Damp silent winds are moving vertical blinds.
Distant chatter from the patio below.

Remembering a betrothal on this twenty-seventh of April.
That spring morning felt like summer's cool heat.
Lilac bridesmaid dresses, flowers and purple ribbons.
White-pearled wedding gown—
All in step with silver-gray tuxedos.

Photos near glass mirrors and redbud cherry trees.
Entering the church as a Miss and walking out a Mrs.
rice thrown with such fervor.
Parents happily crying.
Reminiscing about their children all grown,
and now married.

A day hitting ninety degrees.
Bridal photos—
Kissing when the glasses clinked.
Sitting at the head table.
Now we sit separately looking out our windows.
Sending greetings for a day that no longer exists.

Sifting Through March With an April View

Certainly added disappointments.
Surely need to focus towards other prospects.
No longer heeding to nonsense.
Adding records to the turntables rhythm.
An observation of boats cresting over green waves.
While our capsized boat named Herron was spotted.
What happened to us, now a postmodern hell?
So loud, please decrease the violin tone.
We used to fly kites on the beach,
with momentary words.
We loved to pick up spiraled seashells.
Red views up and behind mountain ridges.
Being a peculiar site and yet so plain.
Obstructions abound across the rocky Pine Barrens.
April's imaginative minds have melded together.

Roses and Thorns

We beat ourselves up, stuck in our mind,
teetering on the fringes of grace.
Thoughts escaping by tapping on meridian points.
We crave nature with heartbreaking poetry.

Juggling hardness of heart…
Wishing for three missing children to forgive.
Sorrow mixed with solitude, as wrens sing under the orange-
yellow sky.
Exhausted and so tired of complaining.

Walking with disappointment on Wednesday.
We are window reflections of our ancestors.
Anxiety is too much,
trying to compensate with hope.
Contemplating the air we are breathing.

So much truth over the lies we speak.
Animals are quiet in a snowy March wind redemption.
Overcoming weedy plants, as blossoms scatter while hiking.
A thought is screaming neither wrong nor right.

Twisted canvas paint of sharp thorns mixed with faded red roses.
We create words that float untamed.
Seeking security and refusing a chaotic modern life.

Blocked

Enjoying what a mind can do of turning thoughts tumbling onto
the page.
My soul is joyful when capturing an audience that appreciates
melodious prose.
Yet every now and then words are too jumbled to express.
Sitting here, my writing is a blur,
my brain fried beyond compare.

Caught up in extreme writer's block is the only frustrating notion.
It feels like a sense of creative direction is lost.
Writing sentence upon sentence,
scribbling and crossing out.
Over and over again.

My paper is more black ink than white paper.
Needing to run away from the writer's desk would be the best
course of action…
Take that walk—
Leave the mental block alone.
The nagging, uncontrollable mind floats away.
To be replaced with clarity upon my return.
With words flowing back onto the parchment.

Facing the Truth

Running away only to regain sanity.
Leaving my dingy white mourning coat,
and a blue bag of lies.

Leaving a roach-infested human disarray.
Four miles of streaming thoughts.
Eighteen months of losing my soul.
Thinking my service was of truth, but instead only lies.
Walking past old industrial buildings.

The bakery and river floodgates.
Walking away from loss,
and misrepresentative endeavors.

Trying to catch my hazy breath, towards my childhood court.
Self-talk of what should have been truth.

While self-doubt creeps in.
Tear and sweat melded together,
riding down my skin.
A fortnight of coping.
Needing to reprogram that monkey mind.

Gas Station Lily

Beauty left unnoticed between Main and Providence.
A lily grows amongst the soot and grime of Bull's Head gas station island.
Cab drivers honking their horns so loudly...
It screams the impatience of our modern society.

As motorists race by to get their next destination.
They only see a mundane traffic light and the price of gas.
Customers run in and out of the convenient store for cigarettes.
Powerball tickets in hand with dreams of winning big.
Not looking up to see nature's glory blooming straight ahead.
Walker, joggers and bicyclists coursing by...

Not a word or a gasp to recognize this miracle.
How could you miss this wondrous star lily?
Her colors ablaze with every shade of pink set off by white.
Boldly presenting herself in the center of our lives.
To admire and proclaim that life is so sublime despite the gravel!

Unpacking a Former Life

Christmas lights and a gifted Nativity set.
Unwrapping a long ago life.
Thinking old feelings were best kept
hidden in attic boxes.
Just the sight of a former name on a box,
brought memories of should haves.
And should have naught.
Feelings overwhelmed by the moments of long ago storms
Feelings of broken isolation—
Hoping the old pains would not return with a furious tornado.
Streaming through tears of reminisce.
Realizing I was stifled,
unable to express my true nature…
Engulfing the hurt and anger of broken lines crossed.
Releasing this burden to a child in the manger.

Free From Sorrow

I write the words on paper that only you can give me.
I am sorry that you had to leave.
I am sorry you left this earth in so much pain.
I am sorry that your eyes witnessed war and strife.
I am sorry that the Green Zone was really not a safe haven.
I am sorry scud missiles made you run for your life.
I am sorry that blood filled the Tigris River.
I am sorry that there was no solace in Baghdad.
I am sorry that you lost your fellow comrades, who were blown
to nothing that day in the barrack's gym.
I am sorry that your Iraqi interpreters will never be seen again, in a
war they never wanted.
I am sorry that when you came home and you had to attend
funerals of your comrades who took their lives.
Because the pain of war was too much to fathom…
I am sorry that PTSD was your new normal.
And that nobody really understood--
I am sorry your life became so full of sorrow.
I am sorry it was so unbearable that leaving us was the only way to
stop this madness.
I am eternally grateful that you protected my sister.
I am eternally grateful that you defended this nation.
I am eternally grateful that you served with honor, distinction and
bravery.
I will count you, my dear amongst the five-pointed golden stars in
the beautiful night sky.

The Defunding of Humanity

I can't...

I just can't participate.
In commentary of another human being's horrid demise.
Demise by the hands of five human beings sworn to "serve and
protect."
I think of Rodney King in this moment, images still emblazoned in
my mind.
A second before shutting off that dreadful noise box invention.
Shaking and shuttering again—
Over a snippet of another beating.
A once vital Tyre—
He is now reduced to battered human rubble.
No one is perfect; this world is not made for perfection.
Police work can be social work.
Ripping apart another's countenance is not a solution.
Solutions are made with clearer thoughts.
Finding ways to garner assistance.
Listening to the Sunday morning broadcast,
And the commentator asking,
Why?
For what?
Are we now back to our post-pandemic lull?
Why is Congress slow to act?
Not listening to the cries of we,
their people.
Maybe they are too busy to comprehend the magnitude of division
in our country.
And yet—
I am writing another prose of protest.
Protesting that my poetry, should not include such atrocities!

The American Hero

The American Hero is one who serves their country.
Despite the fact that war is not always an easy decision.
Because they have chosen honor and duty for their country.
To serve in times of war and to uphold the precepts of peace.
They are the sons and daughters of "one nation under God."
Leaving everything behind and we, the families, are proud of their commitment.
The colors they stand for.
One of red—
For the blood that has been shed by those who valiantly defend America.
One of white—
Symbolizing hope that one day our world will know peace.
Finally one of blue—
For the courage to serve our nation when called upon.
May God's speed keep vigil.
Until you are safely back in Liberty's arms once again.

Dreaming of Reunions

Misunderstood dreams.
Walking down this pitted dirt road.
Golden fields have awakened my attention.
My children are waving from afar.
Trapped in a hazy sea of wheat.
So distant we are now.
And yet I bore my beauties.
Crying through those marvelous tears.
So fiercely loving.
Holding the two of them in my arms.
Recollections of a lifetime ago.
Divorce—
Is far from pretty.
Even after all of these years.
Children suffer no matter what the age.
My lost children don't exist in this realm.
They go back into a greener garden.
To find respite away from their pain.
We will be reunited in that secret garden.
And it will be a reunion of total bliss.
For now I dream the dream of reunion.
Waiting by the pitted dirt road.

An American Wake

(A tribute to Erinn's Lass)

Unable to mourn along the Irish Sea.
So here I walk amongst family graves.
On a brisk winter's night—
Honoring your memory in this outdoor cathedral wake.
Scottish hymns accompany me on this funeral walk.
Remembering your words of welcome.
Somehow you knew—
Of our Wexford return.
Your voice rings through my mind's eye.
Like a soft sea wind.
Laughter and stories are returning.
From the far recesses of the past.
Teaching me to explore every stitch of our heritage.
Knowing our Corish name was integral to Irish history.
Perhaps even a bit of folklore—
Bravely walking around Our Lady's Island.
On that stormy day with Molly.
Walking past ruins of monks and pilgrims.
Wild streams scoring the land.
Reaching the loch to salt waters somewhere in between.
Placing stones on ancient Corish and Kehoe graves.
Singing songs of Wild Roses and Wexford Carols.
Sitting past eleven o'clock as the summer sun was just beyond
Lyra.
Irish air—
The feel of Irish air is like no other.
Encircled with ancestors who keep watch.
Now counting you amongst Celtic angels.
American sunrays are shooting up.
Like columns of fire—
As if your spirit is still walking along.
Still guiding this bard to write your poetic memorial.
Envisioning you smiling down upon me.
Happiness for you is reunion with your beloved Padraig.

Darkness falls—
As this American wake is about to end.
Turning around one last time.
My eyes met an ethereal view.
A view only heaven had orchestrated.

The Alchemy of Kindness

Kindness is the way to find a raised head with a smile.
Shadowy figures love kindness for it feeds their soul.
Like a friend that goes haunting into that heavenly night.
Amongst the feathers he is now lost to the wind.
People do not notice the nuances of life.

The skin is a healing encasement.
Like Italian silk scarves with colors of green and gold.
Walking into this feeble connection.
We may stand alone on this earth.
But we are never really alone by the cypress tree.
Kindness changes misunderstood words.

Into the light of clarity.
We lose and yet remember those dreams.
Those dreams that guide us towards the answers we seek.
Familiar celebrations by the fireplace.
As our children were laughing and playing.
So much kindness—

Leaves will tumble like the sands of time.
Grain by grain.
Leaf by falling leaf, beckoning winter's call.
The earth is famous to those who stop and ponder.
Every child chases fireflies.
The simplicity of childhood needs no introduction.
It is just beauty—

Our vegetable and flower gardens were ripe at harvest.
Making bouquets and potluck suppers.
Their fragrance is kindness to all who entered our kitchens.
Wafting through the neighbor's windows.
Dishes are now falling apart.
Someday those shattered pieces will form a beautiful mosaic.
Of kindness in your honor.
Squinting my eyes from that mysterious light.

Stars shine like iridescent orbs.
The golden act of transforming kindness will be etched.
A never-fading form of spiritual elegance.

Sunday's Departures

Sixty days and these departures are always on Sunday.
Was the Sabbath timely for everyone to depart?
Notices and phones calls of loved ones leaving the train station.
Departures from Ireland—
Texas—
Florida—
New York—
And Scranton.
Trying to console one another as this speeding train moves on.
Past the curtained vale.
Past a soldier's wake.
Past the locked unit of a nursing home.
Past Loch Gorman near Bridgetown South.
Past Polish ancestors.
Past the home of compassion.
I don't want to have time for this train.
We all have tickets in hand awaiting our final destination.
A few close whistle calls made the conductor's platform.
It was not their time yet,
on the train schedule.
I sit here and weep of those who departed the train station.
On God's time…

Anticipation

Parents waiting for newborn birth.
Newborn birth gives way to possibilities.
Possibilities pondered over a child's future.
A child's future is infused with love.
With love, children are free to discover.
Free to discover new ways of learning.
Learning about the world opening up to all opportunities.
Opening up to all opportunities of education.
Education enables many levels of human engagement.
Levels of human engagement foster friendships.
Fostering friendships is a gift.
A gift not wasted by lack of time.
Lack of time and searching for unanticipated moments.
Unanticipated moments are what make life so marvelous.

Raquel

My sleeved heart is doubly broken.
Our beautiful, sweet, black princess has gone to play,
with her sister, Riley.
Your heart could no longer take our sweet angel's passing.
Your sorrow was too much,
for your nineteen-year-old body to bear.
Crying and meowing.
Green eyes filled with grief.
Staring off and searching,
as you slowly slipped away.
Letting us know your time is near.
Hiding under dad's side of the bed.
Not wanting to play with Pumpkin and Dusty.
Cuddling with us one last time,
on the sofa-pillowed edge.
Looking for Riley.
And searching one more time.
Wrapping you up in a soft blue blanket.
Back to the veterinary office, yet again.
Beautiful words of comfort from the staff.
Sitting in the same back room.
Holding your feeble body
next to mine as your heartbeat left.
Your happiness is now our sorrow.
Another empty space,
and another cross in our flower garden.
Pumpkin and Dusty searching for you,
as I opened the office door.
We will be reunited again, my sweet girl.
When we pass through heaven's colored vale.

Anastasia's Tale of Two Harbors

As you left, Great-Grandmother, from the Harbor of Cobh.
I am returning from the Harbor of New York.
Both of us channeling over the vast Atlantic Ocean.
I sit in my comfortable metal cabin.
Yet, you endured a dangerous wooden cabin.
In sorrow leaving your beautiful Irish green land behind.
Anticipation runs through your mind of what America will hold for
you.
As I contemplate what Ireland has in store for me.
Great-Grandmother, was the red, white and blue paved with gold
for you?
Did liberty quell the sorrow of leaving our ancient land?
Or were you served the immigrant's platter of scorn and injustice?
Yet, my greeting was a warm welcome after one hundred and
seventeen years of absence.
It was a grand and glorious reunion.
Great-Grandmother—
Thank you, for the courage to embark on that voyage.
Daughter of Hibernia—
Your legacy is infinitely the muse of this author.

Deconstruction

For I have wounds that are seen and unseen.
Hiding my scars for vanity's sake.
Recalling the pain of how each one came to pass.
Deconstruct me, Lord, for ego and shame inhibit,
the vocation of my higher self.
Hiding behind the false mask of security.
Deconstruct me, Lord, to dispel the falsehood of negativity.
For my inner scars are deeply rooted in the weeping willow
tree.
Weeping over events that are uncontrollable.
Reconstruct me, Lord, so that the wounds may heal.
And claim the true calling of my nature.
Enable me to throw away all pretenses of worldly ways and
worldly means.
Deconstruct me, Lord, and build me up
Brick by brick, filling in those cracks,
as you see fit.
So that I may be your instrument on this earthly stage.
Making sure my actions is loving and joyful.

Love Momentarily Stopped Death Today

Working in the health care field illness is all around; even lunchtime conversations are filled with descriptions of disease. Covering many floors, I meet all types of people including other co-workers. The single word that comes to mind is WHY.

Why I am here? Why can't I get better? Why can't I leave? Why do I have to suffer? Why is my loved one dying? The last question is the hardest to be asked by anyone who has a loved one in a hospital bed. It is truly heartbreaking to watch someone you love slowly fade away into death's arms. Because suffering is a part of the last unknown in this life.

When going from floor to floor, hearing these questions, and since I am not a qualified medical professional. I will give the patient or family member a sympathetic ear. Reassuring them I will speak to my case manager. Reassuring them the case manager will stop by the patient's room to address their concerns.

Leaving the room a silent prayer runs through my mind on their behalf. This is something I have done all my life after speaking to anyone who is in distress.
It was the typical busy day and so looking forward to my lunch break. My co-workers and I sat at the usual table near the gift shop.

Talking about our day and the activities after work. All of a sudden, the cafeteria was a buzz concerning a wedding that will be taking place at 3 pm in the chapel. A wedding in the hospital! We thought we were hearing just a silly rumor.

Until our nursing director, Matt, said, "Yes ladies, there will be a wedding today at 3 pm in the chapel.
The daughter of one of our hospice patients came to see me yesterday. She asked permission to use the chapel so she and her fiancé can get married before anything happens to her dad. The family has invited the entire hospital staff to attend."

No sooner than we thanked Matt for the invitation. Members of the cafeteria staff were rolling carts filled with beautiful white flowers, food and a white wedding cake. We were amazed how quickly everything was coming together. Just like life, it quickly gets away from us. Even though I couldn't attend since our department's caseload doesn't give us the opportunity to breathe.

The stroke of 4:30 pm chimed to clock out and just as I was passing by the chapel, the air of beauty permeated into the hallway. A family mixed with hospital staff celebrating a marriage. Thinking to myself despite all of the uncertainty of our lives. Love momentarily stopped death. No matter what we are going through in the end, it is all about love…

Author's Contact Information

Email address: maryanneabdo@blue-stained-glass.com

Current projects in photography, video and various forms of canvas art can be found at:

Facebook: Mary Anne Abdo/Poet/Author

Word Press: https://bluestainedglass.wordpress.com

Instagram: https://www.instagram.com/maryanne.abdo/

YouTube: maryanneabdo@bluestainedglasspoetry64

For anyone who is struggling with mental health issues, please know there is hope and there is help. Your life means so much to every one of us.

Here are some resources to assist those seeking help and information on mental health and illness:

National Alliance on Mental Illness (NAMI)

www.nami.org/help

NAMI Help Line: 1-800-950-6264 (Monday through Friday, 10 a.m. to 10 p.m. ET)

Text "HelpLine" to 62640

Email: helpline@nami.org

National Institute of Mental Health (NIMH)

www.nimh.nih.gov/health/find-help

988 Suicide & Crisis Lifeline

988lifeline.org

Call or text 988. The Lifeline network provides free 24-hour, confidential support to anyone in suicidal crisis or emotional distress.

Veterans Crisis Line

www.veteranscrisisline.net

Dial 988, then press 1, or text 838255. The Veterans Crisis Line connects service members and veterans in crisis with a trained responder—24 hours a day, 7 days a week.

Thank you to all of those who have purchased this book. For every book sold, a portion of the proceeds will go to a local homeless shelter. Your support means so much to me. I appreciate you!

Fractured Lollipop

www.ingramcontent.com/pod-product-compliance
Lightning Source LLC
Chambersburg PA
CBHW052220090426
42741CB00010B/2612